# WORD
# WATCHER'S
# HANDBOOK

# WORD WATCHER'S HANDBOOK

Including a Deletionary
of the Most Abused and
Misused Words

PHYLLIS MARTIN and friends

**A Center for Media Development, Inc., Book**
DAVID McKAY COMPANY, INC.
New York

*Library of Congress Cataloging in Publication Data*
Martin, Phyllis Rodgers.
    Word watcher's guide:
    A deletionary of the most abused and misused words.
    1. English language—Idioms, corrections, errors.
I. Title.
PE1460.M29        428'.1        76-12741
ISBN 0-679-20354-0
ISBN 0-679-20369-9 pbk.

MANUFACTURED IN THE UNITED STATES OF AMERICA

10 9 8 7 6

*To my parents,*
*Amelia and Wilbur Rodgers,*
*who taught me to love books,*
*and to Bruce,*
*whose love and encouragement*
*enabled me to write this one*

# CONTENTS

# FOREWORD

This is a book about words. It evolved from a "word clinic" I give for just about any group that asks me. Since I am much better at talking about words than writing about them, I am tempted to ask you to read this book aloud. At least let me ask you to think about it as an oral communication that has been set in print in order to reach more people.

I chose the title, *Word Watcher's Handbook: Including a Deletionary of the Most Abused and Misused Words,* to show that the book is a way to acquire a trim vocabulary. By trim I do not mean one that is skinny but one that is in good condition; the words in the Deletionary are fat that should be eliminated. Other sections provide exercise for coordination and tone.

My goal is lofty:

*To save the job seeker from a possible turndown.*
*To improve the job holder's chances for promotion.*
*To inspire the student to master the most important tool he or she will ever use: language.*
*To help everyone to avoid embarrassing mistakes in everyday conversation.*

My ultimate aim is to help every reader delete conversational cholesterol that clogs lines of communication.

A college graduate should manage to lose a minimum of five words. A high-school graduate should manage to lose ten to twenty unwanted words. Younger students and dropouts can lose up to fifty in the first week.

I thank all the people who contributed to this book, some of whom, I am sure, will prefer to remain anonymous—considering the nature of their contributions.

A special thanks to Shirlie, Jay, and Kipp, whose sensitive ears collected many of these examples, and to my husband, Bruce, who willingly accepted the role of critic.

# WORD
# WATCHER'S
# HANDBOOK

# INTRODUCTION

Sue, a college-educated, impeccably dressed young woman, was being interviewed for her first job. "The job sounded just right for me," she was saying. "I couldn't hardly wait to come in and try for it." Suddenly her college training and her faultless grooming no longer mattered. The interview was over. The rest was sheer courtesy.

Pat was enthusiastic about the date she had just accepted with the intriguing man who worked at the record store. As their conversation continued, he said, "Well, I'd better get back to work now. I just snuck out to the phone for a minute." Her enthusiasm died.

How many times have you heard errors like these, as jarring to the ear as static on a radio? You are more aware of the error than of the content of what has just been said. Worst of all, the speaker has no idea that he has made a mistake.

Or perhaps you have heard a word pronounced differently from the way you always thought it was pronounced, and thought, "I wonder if I've been saying that right!" You intend to look it up but somehow never do.

Even if you are a fairly well-read person, with a reasonably good vocabulary, there may be just a few errors you are making that are as painful to some people as the two errors above are to you. As you begin to read through this book, you are very likely to be surprised at the number of errors that have slipped into your everyday speech.

*Word Watcher's Handbook* is divided into three chapters, each designed to attack a specific category of language misuse. The first chapter, the Deletionary, lists words you should remove from your vocabulary, either because they are hackneyed and trite (and may leave a similar impression of you) or because they simply are not words. The worst offenders are harmful to the health of your vocabulary. They're poison—throw them away forever. The second part of the Deletionary is a list of feeble phrases that may have been original at one time but have long ago lost their punch.

Chapter 2, Usage, contains words that are frequently misused. Included in this chapter is the section Unmatched Pairs, which lists pairs of words that sound alike or are frequently confused, with short explanations of which one to use when.

Chapter 3, Pronunciation Pitfalls, is a selection of commonly mispronounced words and an easy-to-read guide to the correct way to say them.

Here is the foolproof method for making sure the boners in this book will never appear in your speech:

As you go through the book, make a flash card for each word you were wrong about or unsure of, following the illustrations on pages 7-9. It may seem like busy work, as you measure and snip the cards and carefully print the words, but do it. You will be rewarded later by the convenience. You will also be more likely to discipline yourself to study words that trouble you—once through the flash cards each day and you're finished. Put those cards out in plain view on your dresser or desk, where they will remind you of their existence. Remember, the task will get shorter each day as you throw away the cards you no longer need.

If you become bored with the flash-card method and like to fool around with tape recorders, try this method for variety: Make a recording of the words you would like to learn, leaving a gap of about five seconds after each word. If it is meaning you are trying to remember, pronounce the word correctly on the tape and give yourself enough time to write down the meaning on a blank sheet of paper before going on. Then compare your paper with the book and grade yourself. If you are working on pronunciation, say into the microphone, "How do you pronounce C-H-A-S-M?" You can write down the correct pronunciations.

You can also simply make a tape of the words that you have trouble pronouncing. Just hearing them over and over again while you wash the dishes or get dressed can help to impress them in your memory. It's best not to record any wrong pronunciations, even for test purposes, because hearing the word mispronounced will hamper your ear training.

Now for a few final touches that will improve your communication with others. Even perfect speech will not be effective unless you keep the listener in mind in the following ways:

• The person with an average vocabulary spends half the conversation time talking with those whose vocabulary is smaller than his. If your vocabulary is larger than average, you are even more likely to be misunderstood. Be sensitive to your audience, whether it's one person or hundreds. If you use a word that you think might be strange to your listeners, use it in a context that reveals its meaning.

• Beware of the sheer length of some words. They are tiring to a listener's ears. If it's clarity of communication that you seek, try plain, sturdy, sure-footed words; then, if you can't resist a long word, your listener will have the strength to absorb it.

• Don't make bounding leaps in your speech, leaving out the essential intermediate steps—or, even worse, filling in with "you knows" and "et ceteras." Be articulate; the listener needs to be carefully led. If you can't express what you mean clearly, imagine how fuzzy the listener's picture will be.

• To keep an audience's attention, make sure your speech is full of visual images. Examples are an excellent means of creating pictures.

• Learn to improve the pitch and volume of your own voice. Listen to yourself on a tape recorder, at least, and take a few voice-training lessons if you think you need it. You can be taught to lower the pitch of your voice, for instance.

• Use your dictionary as those hard-working lexicographers intended. Know that the job of the lexicographer is to REPORT USAGE, not to arbitrate usage. The fact that you see a word in a dictionary does not mean the writers of the dictionary sanction the word in question. That is why many dictionaries contain special "correct usage" or "common error" sections.

• Read, but be careful about trying out new words before you are sure of their pronunciation.

• Go to a lecture now and then instead of a movie.

• Listen to a talk show on the radio, or watch one on television, instead of a situation comedy.

• Remember your normal share of the speaking time is only 50% in a conversation with one other person. It is proportionately less with a larger group. Exceed that share only when you are sure others agree you should.

• Finally, don't allow all these do's and don'ts to ruin brisk, original, pleasant speech. Be spontaneous and say things your way.

## LISTENING

A large part of communicating well is listening well. Listen closely to the others instead of concentrating on what you're going to say next: then what you do say will make more sense. The most polished speech will sound foolish if you are not following the thread of the conversation.

Even more important, when you take the time to hear and understand what the other person is really saying, you save marriages, friendships, and jobs and you learn the true art of communication.

Answer the following questions about yourself, and look back at them after a few weeks to see if you are improving your listening skills.

### Are you a positive listener?

Do you say to the speaker, "Tell me about it"?

Do you give encouragement to the speaker and reassure him from time to time that you are with him?

Do you look at the speaker?

Do you follow the speaker's ideas a little further, asking specific questions and trying to hit on what the speaker's deepest interest in the subject is?

Do you listen for clues to what the speaker's interests are and search for an area of mutual interest?

Do you echo important messages, to make sure you understood them?

### Are you a negative listener?

Do you say to the speaker, "I know just what you're going to say"?

Do you say, "We've tried that before" as soon as he begins an
   explanation, or, just as bad, when he's all finished?

Do you look away from the speaker?

Do you think you know someone else's point of view before he
   tells you?

Do you decide in advance that you know more about the
   subject than the speaker does?

Do you decide ahead of time that the subject is dull? That the
   speaker is dull?

Do you find the merest pretext to turn the conversation back
   to yourself, your preoccupations, or your ideas?

---

Finally, a word of advice that has nothing to do with speaking
or listening: Kind words are more important than the kind of
words you use.

---

# SAMPLE FLASH CARDS

You can use different colors of paper for deletions, definitions, and pronunciations.

## Deletionary

I must delete the phrase
## can't hardly
from my vocabulary

**Front**

The correct phrase is
## can hardly

**Back**

## Usage

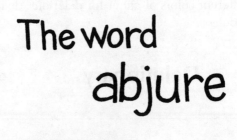

The word
*abjure*
means_____

**Front**

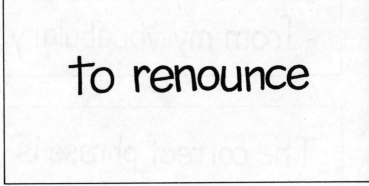

To renounce

**Back**

## Pronunciation

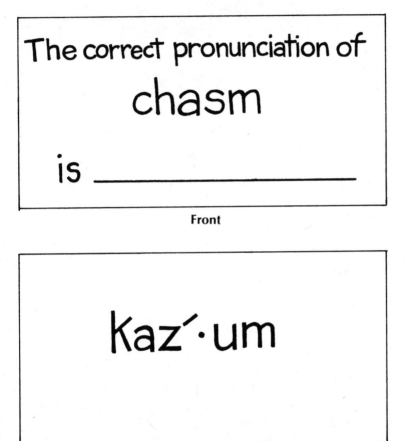

The correct pronunciation of

# chasm

is _____

**Front**

# kaz´·um

**Back**

# 1 / DELETIONARY

When you use too many words, you tire your listener and make it more difficult for him to hear the important words. You can also give the impression that you are fond of the sound of your own voice, when in truth you are just speaking as you are used to speaking, with all the bad habits you have picked up along the way. This chapter will guide you in clearing away the excess words and phrases that are cluttering your speech. It will help to make you into one of those admirable people of whom it is said, "He spoke a few well-chosen words."

Some of the words in the Deletionary are just plain wrong and make a far worse impression of you than verbosity does. If any of the nonwords that follow have crept into your speech, make that flash card now and be sure that when the card is finally thrown away, the nonword is gone forever, too.

The list includes trite and overused expressions as well as wordy and wrong ones. Notice that although old clichés are dreary, there is nothing more warmed-over-sounding than yesterday's slang.

**absolutely**    Don't use this word when you mean "yes."

**accidently**    You mean **accidentally.** Pronounce all five syllables: **ak•si•den′•tahl•lee.**

| | |
|---|---|
| **acrost, acrossed** | The word you want is **across**. |
| **advance planning** | What other kind of planning is there? The same goes for *advance warning*. |
| **afeared** | This is a corruption of the word **afraid**. Please delete it from your vocabulary. |
| **ahold** | Not standard English. Drop the **a**. |
| **ain't** | Colloquial. Is not and are not are preferable. |
| **all things being equal** | What could this possibly mean, when you think about it? |
| **and stuff** | A filler phrase, to make your statement sound more complete than it is. |
| **and that** | Same as *and stuff*. |
| **anyways** | Say **anyway**. |
| **anywheres** | No s here either; it's **anywhere**. |
| **aren't I** | When you use this phrase, you are contracting the words *are I not*. **Am I not** is preferred to *aren't I*. |
| **ascared** | Not standard English. The words are **scared** and **afraid**. |
| **as you know** | If they know, you shouldn't be telling them again. **As you may know** makes more sense, but don't use it just to be polite. |
| **at this point in time** | One of the many verbose phrases that should be replaced by good old **now**. |
| **a whole nother thing** | The word **another** is divided and **whole** is stuck inside. Say instead, **That's another matter entirely,** or if you must be informal, **That's a whole other thing.** |
| **balance** | Don't use this word as a substitute for **rest**, although you may use it when speaking of money: **The balance is due when we pick up the chair.** |
| **basket case** | Not a nice expression, especially if it's used for what it means. |

**beautiful!** Appropriate about once a year.

**beautiful person** Doesn't this phrase imply that everyone else isn't beautiful? *Beautiful person* is passé now, and it's about time. The simple **I like him** has more force than *He's a beautiful person.*

**be that as it may** Archaic- and pedantic-sounding. The word **but** will do.

**blame it on** You can **blame** a person, or **put the blame on** him.

**boughten** A nonword. Use **bought.**

**bretzel** You mean **pretzel;** and it starts with **p.**

**bust** Avoid saying *bust* when you mean **burst.**

**by the same token** Hackneyed. Usually, the word **also** will do fine. If a comparison is being made, be specific.

**can** Don't use as a substitute for **may.** *Can* denotes ability; **may** denotes permission.

**can't hardly** This is a double negative and should not be used. Say **can hardly.**

**case** Don't use as a substitute for **instance** or **example.** *In most cases* should be **In most instances.**

**character** Slang when used to mean a "unique personality."

**charisma** Once a lovely word meaning "a special gift of the Holy Spirit," **charisma** is now applied to everyone from politicians to underground movie stars.

**chauvinist** How about saying, for example, **He's condescending to women?** It's more specific, less rhetorical.

**complected** The word is **complexioned.**

**confrontation** Sometimes **meeting** will do.

| | |
|---|---|
| **consciousness raising** | *Anything* is better; how about "deepening awareness" for the sake of variety? |
| **consensus of opinion** | The idea of "opinion" is built into the word **consensus**. |
| **cool** | An overworked fad word from the fifties. |
| **curiously enough** | Say **curiously**. It's more effective. |
| **disadvantaged** | A euphemism for **poor**. |
| **drapes** | It's **draperies**. |
| **drownded** | The past tense of **drown** is **drowned**. |
| **due to the fact that** | Just say **because**. By the way, only a thing can be **due** to another thing. You cannot say, for instance, **We capsized, due to the heavy wind**; you must say **because of**. |
| **emote** | Not a word. To **show emotion** is the equivalent, or you may be more precise. |
| **encounter** | **Meet?** |
| **enthused** | Not a word. Say **enthusiastic**. |
| **escalate** | There's nothing wrong with this new word, except that it's overused. |
| **estimated at about** | Delete the *about*: that's part of the meaning of **estimate**. |
| **et** | Not a word. Say **we have eaten** or **we ate**—never *we et*. |
| **excape** | The word you want is **escape**. There is no **x** in the word. |
| **expertise** | Use **knowledge** or **experience** for a change. |
| **famed** | A self-conscious coinage by the mass media, as if to say, "He's famed, and *we* famed him." **Famous** is still much preferred. |
| **fantastic** | Overworked. Try **fanciful, odd, grotesque**. When it is used to express vague positive feelings, it is sadly misused. |

| | |
|---|---|
| finalize | Finish, complete, conclude? |
| flustrated | A combination of flustered and frustrated? Be precise, and use one or the other. |
| for free | Free or for nothing are fine, but *for free* sounds childish. |
| frame of reference | Background? Viewpoint? Academic discipline? |
| gent | Say gentlemen or man. |
| gross | Overused. Try vulgar or coarse. |
| growth | To those who laud all "growth," I say, "Remember cancer and kudzu." |
| guesstimate | Means "a very rough estimate"? Say so. *Guesstimate* may have been mildly amusing the first time it was used. |
| heartrendering | If you must use this tired expression, make it heartrending. You render fat, not hearts. |
| heighth | Not a word. The term you want is height. Pronounce it hite (rhymes with kite). |
| hinderance | Though derived from the word hinder, this verb's noun form is hindrance, and it has only two syllables. |
| hisself | Not a word. The correct word is himself. |
| hopefully | Say I hope or even plain old perhaps: the hope is sometimes evident in the context. |
| how about that? | A tired old nonremark. |
| hunnert | The word you want is hundred. |
| I been | Say I have been. |
| I done | I have done, or I did. |
| I don't think | How can you express an opinion if you don't think? Try "I think not." The phrase "I don't think" hurts many ears. |
| incidently | The word is incidentally, and it has five syllables. |

| | |
|---|---|
| **in my opinion, I think** | **I think** is sufficient. *In my personal opinion* is of the same order. |
| **insightful** | Overused. Try **discerning, intuitive, penetrating.** |
| **irregardless** | The word is **regardless.** |
| **it don't** | This is a contraction of *it do not,* an incorrect phrase. Say **it does not** or **it doesn't.** |
| **learning experience** | One either learns from experience or one doesn't; the phrase is meaningless. |
| **love** | If **like** will do, you're using the word **love** too loosely. |
| **marginal** | When used in phrases such as *a marginal difference,* the word means nothing that **small** doesn't mean. Unless you're referring to a margin, say **small.** |
| **meaningful dialogue** | This phrase usually expresses a vague, positive feeling toward the dialogue when the speaker cannot verbalize what was said. Try asking yourself, What was the meaning of the dialogue? |
| **meaningful experience** | Same problem: What was the meaning of the experience? |
| **meaningful relationship** | *Both* words are usually euphemisms here. |
| **muchly** | Avoid. This word was all right in Shakespeare's time, but it is considered affected and incorrect today. |
| **my personal opinion** | If it's your opinion, then by definition it's personal. |
| **needless to say** | A filler. If it were needless, you wouldn't be saying it. |
| **never before in the past** | Pick one: **before** or **in the past.** |

**nowheres**    The word is **nowhere** (without the **s**).

**off of**    Omit the *of*. **Get off the bus.**

**okay?**    When used intermittently in a narrative, this word annoys the listener by begging for his approval.

**ongoing**    Most sentences featuring *ongoing* are strengthened by omitting it.

**orientate**    Not a word. Say **orient**.

**oughta**    Not standard English. Say **ought to** or **should**.

**out loud**    **Aloud** is preferred.

**out of**    Use with care. In some phrases the *of* is superfluous, as in *look out of the window* or *walk out of the door.* Unless you're a termite, make that **out the door.** You can only get out of something you have been in; i.e., you can **walk out of a building.**

**overly**    The prefix **over-** sounds better, or just say too.

**over with**    Omit the *with*.

**personal friend**    In most instances, **friend** is enough.

**personally, I think**    Same as *my personal opinion*—the *personally* is unnecessary.

**plastic**    Let's return this one to its dictionary meaning, and to all "plastic" parents: may your offspring think of something more original.

**please?**    If you're speaking German, you're allowed to say, *Bitte?* ("Please?"), meaning, "what did you say?" Since many people do not understand this colloquialism, in English it is better to avoid it. Then, too, there are many who understand it but can't stand it.

**presently**   If you mean "now," say **now**. You may use **presently** to mean "soon," but **soon** is shorter and less pretentious.

**prior to**   Say **before**.

**quote**   Correct as a verb (**He quoted Emerson**) but not as a noun (say **a quotation from Emerson**).

**rap**   For "talk," a little shopworn.

**really**   If you're using it for emphasis, rather than to mean "as opposed to appearances," eliminate it.

**relatively**   **Relatively** can be nothing but an attempt to get yourself off the hook when you think you've said something too definite. If you can't say what's relative to what, chances are nothing is, and you should leave this word out. *Relatively speaking* almost always means nothing.

**relevant**   The word relevant appears in this section because so many people complained that they are tired of hearing it. You may want to say **pertinent** or **to the point**.

**reoccur**   The correct word is **recur**.

**rewarding**   Try to name what the rewards are.

**right on!**   Originally a political rallying cry, and now misused to express approval of what has just been said. This phrase is tired anyway and would best be marched right on out.

**Sahara desert**   Sahara means "desert," so just say **the Sahara**. The same goes for *Rio Grande River* and *Mt. Fujiyama* (it's the **Rio Grande** and **Fujiyama**, or **Mt. Fuji**).

**see what I mean?**   Another phrase, like *okay?*, that begs approval.

| | |
|---|---|
| **snuck** | Not standard English. Say **sneaked.** |
| **spastic** | A word that is offensive except when correctly used as a medical term. |
| **start off** | Just say **start.** You don't need *off* after it. |
| **supposing** | The word is **suppose,** as in, "Suppose you go first." |
| **swang** | Dialectical past tense form of **swing. Swung** is preferred. |
| **tell it like it is** | Old as old slang. |
| **thanking you, I remain** | Old and trite. |
| **that fact *is*, is that** | This phrase is wholly unnecessary, but the double **is** sounds tongue-tied besides. |
| **theirselves** | The word is **themselves.** |
| **this here** | If the object or person referred to is present, **this** alone is enough. If it's not present, substitute **a** for **this.** Say **A boy I met at the beach,** not *This boy I met at the beach.* |
| **thusly** | Say simply **thus.** |
| **umble** | The word is **humble.** Sound the **h.** |
| **unawares** | No. The word should not have an **s.** Say **unaware.** |
| **unbeknownst** | Pompous substitute for **unknown.** |
| **underprivileged** | Say **poor** instead. |
| **undoubtably** | The word is **undoubtedly,** pronounced **un•dow′•ted•lee.** |
| **valid** | A tired word. Try **Cogent. Well-grounded. Solid. Genuine.** |
| **viable** | **Possible, capable of living, alive?** |
| **widow woman** | **Widow** is sufficient. The word already encompasses the idea of woman, just as widower includes the idea of man. |

**-wise**   As a handy suffix, meaning "in any way whatsoever related to the root word," **-wise** is misused.

**you can say that again**   Conversational overkill. You can nod politely to show that you agree.

**you know**   A hedge for when the speaker doesn't know how to explain something. "You know" can get to be an annoying habit; better to eliminate it altogether.

**youse**   Please rid your vocabulary of this nonword. The plural of **you** is **you.**

# Runners-Up

Before we leave this section of the chapter, let me mention that almost everyone dislikes professional jargon, "trendy" words, and "buzz" words. Teachers complain about social workers, doctors about lawyers—you get the idea: nobody wants to be on the outside of a discussion.

Take a look at this list of runners-up in the Most Overused Words contest. You don't have to delete these words from your vocabulary entirely, but check to see that you are not giving some of them more than their fair share of the air waves.

alienated
articulate (as a verb)
awesome
bizarre
climate (other than the weather variety)
concept
controversial
credibility
depersonalization
dialogue
dynamics
elegant
enrichment
exciting
holistic
involved
manic
obscene

operative
oppressed
overreact
paranoid
politicized
posture (for "attitude")
priorize
rationalize
rhetoric
rip-off
scenario
share
structure (as a verb)
substantive
superlative
thrust
ventilate (feelings)
veritable

# FEEBLE-PHRASE FINDER

Many of the following phrases once evoked vivid images; some were downright poetic. But now they slip out automatically—"as a bee" following "busy" before we can stop ourselves. They evoke nothing in the listener except weariness.

You have a right to know how I compiled this list. And if you're thinking, "My, doesn't she have her nerve?" I'll agree with you. It takes nerve. Especially since a few of my favorite expressions are included.

I believe I started this back in Freshman English at the University of Cincinnati. And I know I used such a list for a secretarial program I led at the executive offices of Procter & Gamble. I know, too, that all of us in personnel agreed to help each other "banish the bromide."

Naturally, an updated version of that list became a part of my current Word Watchers' Clinic. But the collection you see here has many contributors: my family, friends, teachers, business associates, and every person who has been part of the word clinic.

I don't stand in front of the class spieling off what I think are hackneyed phrases. Participants tell me—on cards provided or by taking the floor and telling the class and me. They also tell me by phone. Or mail. And by sending word with those who sign for later sessions.

Only after many people have commented negatively on a trite expression does it "make the list." Each phrase you see had numerous nay votes. "You know" garnered more nay votes than all the other phrases combined. Perhaps you noticed that "Dear Abby" recently devoted a column to the "you know" epidemic.

These canned similes, platitudes, bromides, clichés, and old saws are long overdue for oblivion. Won't you give them the rest they deserve?

abreast of the times
absence makes the heart grow
    fonder
ace in the hole
accidents will happen
acid test
according to one's lights
add insult to injury
after all is said and done
age before beauty
a good time was had by all
all in all
all is not gold that glitters
all too soon
all to the good
all walks of life
all wool and a yard wide
all work and no play
almighty dollar
along the line
also-ran
any and all
apple-pie order
arms of Morpheus
as a whole
as for me
asleep at the switch
as luck would have it
as the crow flies
auspicious occasion
avoided like the plague
back to the drawing board

banker's hours
bark up the wrong tree
bated breath
bathed in tears
bat out of hell
battle for life/of life
beard the lion in his den
beat a dead horse
beat a hasty retreat
bee in her bonnet
beg to advise
believe you me
best bib and tucker
best-laid plans of mice and men
better late than never
better to have loved and lost
bird in the hand
bite off more than one can
    chew
bite the bullet
bite the dust
bitter end
black as coal
blanket of snow
blood is thicker than water
blow off steam
blow your own horn
blow your top
blushing bride
bolt from the blue
born with a silver spoon
bosom of the family

bottom of the barrel
brain trust
break the ice
break your neck
breathe a sigh of relief
bright and early
bright-eyed and bushy-tailed
bright future
bring home the bacon
bring to a head
bring up the rear
briny deep
brown as a berry
budding genius
bundle of nerves
burning question
burn the midnight oil
burn your bridges
bury the hatchet
busman's holiday
busy as a bee
butter-and-egg man
butterflies in the stomach
by hook or crook
by the skin of the teeth
by the sweat of his brow
callow youth
calm before the storm
can't fight City Hall
can't make head nor tail of
carry the ball
cash on the barrel
cast your lot with
cast your pearls before swine
caught red-handed
change your tune
checkered career
chip off the old block

clean as a whistle
clear as a bell
clear as crystal
clear as mud
coals to Newcastle
cock-and-bull story
cold as ice
cold feet
cold sweat
come in out of the rain
come out in the wash
consensus of opinion (redundant
    as well as tiresome)
conspicuous by his absence
contents noted
cool as a cucumber
crack the whip
crash the gate
crooked as a dog's hind legs
crow to pick
crucial third-down situation
cry for the moon
cry over spilt milk
cry wolf
curiously enough (you don't
    need the enough)
cut the mustard
dead as a doornail
dead giveaway
deaf as a post
demon rum
depths of despair
devil to pay
diamond in the rough
did a number
didn't know enough to come in
    out of the rain
didn't know from Adam

didn't lift a finger
die is cast
dirty old man
distance lends enchantment
distinguished speaker
don't put all your eggs in one
    basket
don't take any wooden nickels
doomed to disappointment
doting parent
down in the mouth
down my alley
draw the line
drop in the bucket
drown his sorrow
drunk as a skunk
dull thud
during the time that
dyed in the wool
each and every
eager beaver
early on
ear to the ground
easier said than done
eat, drink, and be merry
eat your hat
eleventh hour
enclosed please find
everything went along nicely
exception proves the rule
explore every avenue
eyeball to eyeball
eyes bigger than one's stomach
eyes like saucers
eyes like stars
eyes of the world
face the music
fair sex

far be it from me
far cry
fast and loose
fat's in the fire (a favorite of the
    late Erle Stanley Gardner—
    he could get by with it)
feather in his cap
feel his oats
few and far between
few well-chosen words
field of endeavor
fill the bill
filthy lucre
fine and dandy
first and foremost
first pop out of the box
fish or cut bait
fish out of water
flash in the pan
flat as a pancake
flat on your back
flip your lid
flog a dead horse
fly-by-night
fly in the ointment
fly off the handle
fond farewell
fools rush in
foreseeable future
for my part
for the pure and simple reason
free as the air
fresh as a daisy
from rags to riches
frozen stiff
frying pan into the fire
gainfully employed (you don't
    need the gainfully)

gala occasion
game plans
garden variety
gentle as a baby
gentle as a lamb
get in one's hair
get it off your chest
get the sack
get to the point
get your dander up
gild the lily
give a piece of your mind
give short shrift to
give the gate
glad rags
go against the grain
God's country
gone to seed
good as gold
good as new
go scot-free
got his number
go to pieces
go to the dogs
got the upper hand
got up on the wrong side of the
   bed
grain of salt
graphic account
greatness thrust upon
green as grass
green with envy
Grim Reaper
grin like a Cheshire cat
ground below (Since the ground
   is usually below, you
   probably don't need to say
   below.)

gum up the works
had the privilege
hail fellow well met
hair of the dog
hair's breadth
halcyon days
hale and hearty
half a mind to
hammer and tongs
hand in glove
hand to mouth
handwriting on the wall
hang by a thread
hang in there, baby
happy as a lark
hard as nails
hard row to hoe
has a screw loose
has-been
have another think coming
haven't seen you in a coon's age
head and shoulders above
head over heels
heart in my mouth
heart of gold
heart of hearts
hem and haw
herculean task
hide your light under a bushel
high-handed
high on the hog
hit below the belt
hit the nail on the head
hit the sack
hit your head against a stone
   wall
hold a candle to
hold the bag

hold the phone
hold your horses
hold your peace
holier than thou
hook, line, and sinker
hook or crook
hornet's nest
horns of a dilemma
horse of a different color
hungry as a bear
I can't believe I ate the whole thing
if and when
if the shoe fits
if you follow me
ignorance is bliss
I'll buy that
I'll drink to that
in a pleasing manner
in a tight spot
in cahoots with
in conclusion would state
in full swing
in my judgment
in no uncertain terms
in one ear and out the other
in other words
in our midst (incorrect and misquoted—see Matthew XVIII)
inspiring sight
in spite of the fact that
institution of higher learning
interesting to note
intestinal fortitude
in the final analysis
in the know
in the last analysis

in the light of
in the long run
in the midst of
in the same boat
in this day and age
in touch with
irons in the fire
irony of fate
it depends on whose ox is being gored
it goes without saying
it's a whole new ball game
it stands to reason
Johnny-come-lately
Johnny-on-the-spot
joined together
join the club
jumping-off place
jump the gun
jump to conclusions
just bear with me
just to inform you
keep a stiff upper lip
keep the pot boiling
keep your eye on the ball
kick in the teeth
know the ropes
lady of leisure
land-office business
last but not least
last straw
law unto herself
lead-pipe cinch
lean and hungry look
lean over backward
leap in the dark
leave in the lurch
leave no stone unturned

left-handed compliment
legend in his own time
let it all hang out
let's face it
let the cat out of the bag
let your hair down
level with me
lick into shape
light as a feather
like a bump on a log
like a lead balloon
limp as a rag
little did I think when
little old lady
lit up like a Christmas tree
live and let live
live high off the hog
live in hopes that
live it up
live off the fat of the land
loaded for bear
lock, stock, and barrel
long arm of the law
long time no see
look a gift horse in the mouth
lose your marbles
lose your shirt
lot of laughs
lucky stiff
lump in the throat
mad as a wet hen
make a clean breast of it
make a long story short/make a
    long story longer
make a mountain out of a
    molehill
make a pitch
make ends meet

make hay while the sun shines
make it perfectly clear
make no bones
make short work of
make the air blue
make the rounds (unless you're
    a doctor)
make things hum
master of all he surveys
may be favored
mean no offense
meets the eye
meets with your approval
method in his madness
might and main
mind your p's and q's
misery loves company
missed the boat
momentous decision
moot point
moot question
more easily said than done
more than meets the eye
more than she bargained for
more the merrier
motley crew
mute testimony
my bag
my door is always open
nagging headache
nail to the cross
naked truth
near at hand
near future
near miss
neat as a bandbox
necessary evil
neck and neck

neck of the woods
needle in a haystack
needs no introduction
neither fish nor fowl
neither rhyme nor reason
never a dull moment
never in the history of
never too late
new broom sweeps clean
new lease on life
new wine in old bottles
nipped in the bud
no expense has been spared
no great shakes
no man in his right mind
none the worse for wear
no place like home
no reflection on you, but
no respecter of persons
nose out of joint
no skin off my nose
no strings attached
not a leg to stand on
not by a long shot
nothing succeeds like success
nothing to sneeze at
nothing ventured
not to be sneezed at
not to exceed
not wisely but too well
not worth a Continental
not worth the paper it's written
    on
no way
nth degree
number is up
of a high order
off the record

of the first order
of the first water
old as Methuselah
old as the hills
old before his time
old head on young shoulders
old stomping/stamping ground
on all fours
on cloud nine
one and only
one and the same
on Easy Street
on the level
on the mark
on the ragged edge
on top of the world
opportunity knocks but once
other fish to fry
other side of the coin
ours is not to reason why
out in left field
out of sight, out of mind
out of sorts
out of the mouths of babes
out of the woods
over a barrel
over the hill
ox to the slaughter
package solutions
pain in the neck
painting the town
pale as a ghost
part and parcel
pass the buck
pass the time of day
pave the way for
pay the piper
peer group

penny for your thoughts
period of time
perish the thought
personal growth
pet peeve
Philadelphia lawyer
picture of health
piece of your mind
pillar of society
pillar to post
pinch hitter
pin it on her/him
pipe dream
plan your work and work your
   plan
play a waiting game
play both ends against the
   middle
play fast and loose
play into the hands of
play it by ear
play to the grandstand
play up to
play with fire
play your cards right
point with pride
poor as a church mouse
power corrupts
powers that be
present company excepted
pretty as a picture
pretty kettle of fish
primrose path
protests too much
pull chestnuts from the fire
pull the wool over his/her eyes
pull up stakes
pull your leg

pull your own weight
pull yourself together
pure and simple
pure as the driven snow
put a bug in his ear
put on the dog
put on your thinking cap
put our heads together
put that in your pipe and smoke
   it
put the bite on
putty in his/her hands
put up job
put your cards on the table
put your foot down
put your foot in it
put your foot in your mouth
put your hand to the plow
put your shoulder to the wheel
quick as a bunny
quick as a flash
quick as a wink
rack and ruin
rack your brain
raining cats and dogs
raise the dead
raise your sights
rake over the coals
ran circles around
rank has its privileges
rattle the wrong cage
read between the lines
read him/her like a book
read the riot act
really and truly
red as a beet
red-carpet treatment
rich as Croesus

rich beyond your wildest
 dreams
ride the gravy train
ride roughshod over
right man in the right place
right on the head
right up my alley
ring a bell
ring true
ripe old age
rise to the occasion
rock of Gibraltar
roll out the red carpet
room at the top
rose-colored glasses
rough and ready
rough and tumble
round of applause
rub the wrong way
run for your money
run-of-the-mill
run up a red flag
sacred cow
sad but true
sadder but wiser
sad to tell
sail under false colors
same the whole world over
same wave length
save for a rainy day
save your breath
save your own skin
sawdust trail
school of hard knocks
seal his doom
sea of faces
see a man about a dog
see beyond the nose on her face

seek his fortune
seek his own level
see my way clear
see the light of day
seething mass of humanity
self-made man
sell him a bill of goods
sell like hot cakes
senior citizens (this has some
 defenders)
set the world on fire
set up shop
set your cap for
set your heart upon
seventh heaven
shadow of a doubt
shadow of his/her former self
shake a leg
shake a stick at
shake in my boots
shape of things to come
share these thoughts/words
shed a little light on the subject
she's on cloud nine
shoot the breeze
shoot the works
short and sweet
shot in the arm
shoulder to the wheel
sibling rivalry
sick and tired
sigh of relief
sight for sore eyes
sight to behold
sight unseen
sign of the times
silence is golden
silent as the grave

since time immemorial
sing like a bird
sink or swim
sitting pretty
sixes and sevens
six of one and half dozen of the
    other
skate on thin ice
skin alive
skin and bones
skin deep
skirt around the edge of
slowly but surely
small world
smart money
smelled like a rose
snake in the grass
snowed under
sock it to me
soft as snow
soft shoulder to cry on
soft spot in his/her heart
so help me Hannah
some kind of
something else
something's rotten in Denmark
so sue me
sound the trumpets
sow wild oats
spanner in the works
split hairs
spread yourself too thin
square meal
square peg in a round hole
square your conscience
stand on your own two feet
stand your ground
start from scratch

staying power
steal a march
steal your thunder
stick around a while
stick-in-the-mud
stick in your craw
stick to the ribs
stick to your guns
stick your neck out
stiff necked
stiff upper lip
still waters run deep
stock in trade
straight and narrow
straight as an arrow
straight from the horse's mouth
straight from the shoulder
strange as it seems
strange but true
strangely enough (just strangely
    will do)
straw in the wind
street of dreams
strike it rich
strike while the iron is hot
strike your fancy
string along with
strong as an ox
struck dumb
stubborn as a mule
stuff and nonsense
stuffed shirt
subsequent to
sum and substance
sumptuous repast
sun drenched
supreme sacrifice
sweeten the kitty

swing a deal
tables are turned
take a back seat
take a leaf out of one's book
take a shine to
take it easy
take it lying down
take stock in
take the liberty
talk through your hat
telling blow
tell it to the Marines
tell tales out of school
tender mercies
that is to say
that's it in a nutshell
the best-laid plans
the foreseeable future
theirs not to reason why
the proud professor
there's a method in his madness
the very nature of things
the wheels of the gods grind
    slowly
the whole ball of wax
thick as thieves
thick-skinned
thin as a rail
think tank
thin-skinned
this side of the grave
those with whom we come in
    contact
through thick and thin
throw a wrench in the
    machinery
throw in the sponge
throw in the towel

throw the book at
time hangs heavy
time immemorial
time is of the essence
time was ripe
tiny tots
tired as a dog
tired but happy
tit for tat
to all intents and purposes
toe the mark
to gird up one's loins
to make a long story short
tongue in cheek
too funny for words
too many irons in the fire
too numerous to mention
tooth and nail
top drawer
to play ball with
to string along
to tell the truth
to the bitter end
to the manner born
touch with a ten-foot pole
tough act to follow
tough as nails
tread lightly
trials and tribulations
trip the light fantastic
true blue
true facts (facts are true)
try men's souls
truth to tell
turnabout is fair play
turn a hand
turn back the clock
turn over a new leaf

turn the tables
turn up your nose
two strings to your bow
ugly as sin
ugly duckling
unable to see the forest for the
    trees
undercurrent of excitement
under the wire
uneasy truce
unless and until
untiring efforts
up against it
ups and downs
value system
vast concourse
view with alarm
viselike grip
wait on hand and foot
walk a tightrope
walks of life
warm as toast
warm the cockles of one's
    heart
wash one's dirty linen in public
wash one's hands of it
water under the bridge
water over the dam
way out
way to go
weaker sex
wee small hours

wended their way
whipping boy
white as a sheet
wide of the mark
wide open spaces
wild oats
win your spurs
wishy-washy
with a high hand
with all my heart
with a vengeance
with bated breath
with might and main
without a doubt
without a prayer
without rhyme or reason
wolf in sheep's clothing
wonderful world of __
word to the wise
world is his oyster
worse for wear
worthy opponent
would I lie to you?
wreathed in smiles
wrong end of the stick
yellow-bellied
you know
you'd better believe it
your guess is as good as mine
your kind indulgence
you've come a long way, baby

# 2 / USAGE

Once you have removed the static from your communications systems by eliminating all the words that are wrong, you can then improve your image even further by following these two rules:

*1. Don't be afraid to use the correct word. It may sound a little stilted to you, or strange, but most of the strangeness is due to the fact that you haven't used the word before. Or if you have, you haven't used it correctly. Don't avoid the word; learn its meaning and then use it.*

*2. Never talk down to those around you by using errors in your own speech.*

| | |
|---|---|
| **aggravate** | To make worse, to increase, as in to aggravate a condition. Do not use when you mean **irritate** or **annoy**. **I am irritated** rather than *I am aggravated.* |
| **agree to, agree with** | You agree to a plan or suggestion and agree with a person. One thing agrees with another thing. |
| **almost** | "Not quite." Do not say *most* for **almost. Almost everybody was there.** |

**alternative**  Some careful speakers and writers insist that there can be only two **alternatives** in any situation. If there are more, they become **choices** or **possibilities**. Some, on the other hand, say that if you *have* to choose one of them, they are **alternatives**, no matter how many there are.

**among**  Use **among** when referring to three or more items. Use **between** if there are only two. **Between you and me. Among the three of us.** In very rare instances, **between** may be proper with more than two, as when the action described can only take place between two of the several at one time.

**amount**  Use **amount** to refer to a general quantity. **There was a large amount of work to be done.** Use **number** to refer to items that can be counted.

**and**  Do not use this word when you mean **to;** for example, **come to see me,** not *come and see me.* See TRY AND.

**angry**  One is angry **at** a situation but angry **with** a person.

**anxious**  "To be worried, apprehensive." Do not confuse with **eager,** wanting something very much.

**anyplace**  Careful speakers and writers avoid this term as a substitute for **anywhere.** In sentences such as **We couldn't find any place to park,** it is two words.

**as**  Equally, in the same manner. **As** is correct before a phrase. **She thinks as I do.** Do not substitute *like,* which is used before nouns or pronouns. See LIKE.

**at**    This word should not be used at the end of a sentence starting with **where.** Say **where is the book,** not *where is the book at.*

**balance**    Used in accounting or to describe a state of equilibrium. When your meaning is *the rest of*, use **remainder.** When speaking of money, you may say **The balance is due when we pick up the chair.**

**barely**    Guard against using with other negative words, as **barely** is already negative, and two negatives cancel each other. Say **can barely,** not *can't barely.*

**basis**    Remember that the plural form is **bases,** pronounced **bay'•seez.**

**beside**    "At the side of, alongside." Do not use *of* after it. **The chair is beside the desk.** Compare with BESIDES.

**besides**    In addition to, as well as. **He has plenty to do besides study.**

**be sure and**    **Be sure to** is the correct form.

**between**    Say **between you and me,** never *between you and I.* See also AMONG.

**bi-weekly**    This tricky word can mean "twice a week" or even "every two weeks," so we never know what to believe when we see or hear it. In your own speech, it's better to use **bi-weekly** for "every two weeks" and **semi-weekly** for "twice a week."

**boat**    "A small vessel." An oceanliner, or any other big vessel, is not a *boat* but a **ship.**

**both alike**    Say simply **they are alike.** You don't need the *both.*

**bring**    In the sense of conveying, **bring** indicates movement toward the speaker. Example:

**Bring the book to me.** The sentence *Bring this form when you go to the doctor's office* is wrong. It should be **take.**

bust

Avoid saying *bust* when you mean **burst.**

but

This word is not needed after *doubt* and *help.* Say **I don't doubt that** rather than *I don't doubt but that.*

check into, check out

Usually **check** is sufficient.

claim

This word is not to be used as a substitute for **say.** Wrong: *She claimed I did it.* Right: **She said I did it.**

class

Do not use this word to describe style (it shows a lack of it). *She really has class* shows that the speaker has none.

clean, clear

These words should not be used to describe degree. *Clean up to here* and *clear up to here* should be eliminated.

come

Do not use this word instead of **came.** The past tense of *come* is came. **I came to the party early.**

come and

Say **come to: Come to see me tomorrow.**

compare with, compare to

**Compare with** is used with two things or people of equal stature, perhaps to point out differences. **Compare to** means "liken to" and is used for fanciful comparisons: **"Shall I compare thee to a summer's day?"** Or: **He compared his teacher to Socrates.**

comptroller

A variant of the word **controller.** Used as the title for a financial officer. Pronounce the same as **controller.**

convince

**Convince** is used with **of** or **that.** Avoid using with *to.* One may persuade someone to do something—in fact, **persuade** can be used with all three constructions.

**couple**    We need to exercise care in the pluralization of this word. Say two couples, not *two couple.*

**crass**    The original and still preferred meaning here is "stupid." The word sounds like **brassy, gross,** and **crude,** but these are very new meanings.

**criterion, criteria**    A **criterion** is a standard test by which something is compared or measured. The plural is **criteria,** often used incorrectly as the singular.

**datum, data**    The word **datum,** rarely used, means a fact. The plural form is **data.** Although **data** is widely used for both the singular and plural, it is comforting to know the difference.

**decimate**    This is from the Latin *decem,* "ten." It means, literally, to "select by lot and kill one in every ten." Many people use it incorrectly to mean "the killing of a large number," or "total destruction."

**did, done**    Avoid *I have did.* Say simply, **I did.** The word **have** must be followed by **done,** as in **I have done my work.** Likewise, never say *I done,* as **done** must not be used alone.

**differ**    Differ **with** a person; differ **from** something; differ **on** an issue.

**different**    **Different from** is the correct form. *Different than* is to be avoided, although **other than** is all right.

**discover**    Do not use interchangeably with **invent. Discover** means "to learn of"; **invent** means "to originate."

**distrust**    "Lack of trust." It has the same meaning as mistrust.

**done**  Not interchangeable with **finish.** If you say **The painting will be done next week,** it is unclear whether you mean "someone will be painting next week," or "by next week the painting will be completed."

**disinterested**  "Impartial, objective." A judge should be a **disinterested** listener. (He should not take sides.) If you mean "having no interest in," say **uninterested. He was an uninterested student; he did a lot of daydreaming.**

**draught**  Chiefly British. Pronunciation and meaning identical to **draft.**

**drug**  This is not the past tense of **drag. Say dragged. She dragged the child out of the room.**

**each**  A singular word. When used in a sentence it must be matched with other singular words. Say **each brought his own** (not *their own*). Since **their** is plural, it is correctly used as follows: **They brought their own.** The plural **their** matches the plural **they.**

**eager**  "Desirous of something." Do not confuse with ANXIOUS.

**end product**  Just say **product** (unless you need to distinguish something from an intermediate product).

**enough**  Guard against inserting *enough* when it is not needed. *We were fortunate enough to receive the gift* is strengthened by saying simply, **We were fortunate to receive the gift.**

**et**  Not to be used when you mean **eaten.** Say **we have eaten,** never *we et.*

**et cetera**  Never say *and et cetera. Et* is Latin for **and.**

**everybody . . . their**  Everybody is still singular and takes a singular pronoun: **Everybody had his or her own umbrella at last.** If that elaborate **his or her** bothers you, say **We all had our own** or **They all had their own.**

**everyplace**  Not when you mean **everywhere.** In sentences such as **Every place was taken,** it is two words.

**except**  You'll do all right if you remember to use **me, him,** and **her** after **except,** in sentences such as "No one loved you except me," and, similarly, "No one loves him except her."

**feel**  When used as a substitute for **think** or **believe,** make sure it fits the context better, and you are not using it just to hedge.

**female**  When referring to human beings, do not use this word as a noun. You may refer to a **group of women,** but not to a *group of females.* It is all right to refer to animals as **females.**

**fewer**  An adjective meaning "a smaller number." Say **there are fewer children in school,** not *there are less children.* See LESS.

**fit**  The past tense of this verb is **fitted.**

**flammable, inflammable**  **Flammable** and **inflammable** are the same in usage and meaning. See NONFLAMMABLE. (One oil company avoids the problems by putting "COMBUSTIBLE" on the sides of its trucks.)

**foot/feet**  It is all right to say **a six-foot rug.** But a man is **six feet tall,** not *six foot.*

**former**  Use **former** to refer to the first of two things. Use **first** to refer to the first of more than two things. **Nicky Hilton was Elizabeth Taylor's first husband.**

**froze**   Do not say *I am froze*. Say either **I froze** or **I am frozen.**

**gal**   Many women are campaigning against the use of the word *gal*. Woman is preferred.

**gift**   By definition, a gift is free. Do not say *a free gift*.

**give**   The past tense of this word is **gave. I gave it to him yesterday.** Never, never say *I have gave*. When paired with **have**, the correct form is **given. I have given it to him.**

**good/well**   Instead of getting into the *I feel good/I feel well* dilemma, say **I am well.** It's easier.

**got**   Do not use when you mean **have.** Wrong: *I got my book with me.* Right: **I have my book with me.**

**graduate**   You can **graduate from a school,** or **be graduated from a school.** You cannot *graduate it*, however, unless you have been given the responsibility of dividing it into grades. *He graduated high school* shows that the speaker probably did not.

**grammatical**   "According to the rules of grammar." Accordingly, we don't say *grammatical errors* but, rather, **errors in grammar.**

**hanged**   A man is **hanged.** A picture is **hung.**

**hardly**   Guard against using with other negative words; **hardly** is already negative. And two cancel each other. Say **can hardly,** not *can't hardly*.

**home**   Not to be used interchangeably with house. The latter refers to a dwelling. Sometimes a home can be created there.

**human**   Pronounced **hyoo'•mun,** this is an adjective, often describing the word **being,** as in **human being.** *Human* as a noun is common only in science fiction. (Sound the **h.**)

**hung**   A picture is **hung.** A man is **hanged.**

**I**   Use **I** only as the subject of a sentence—(**I like this**) or after **is** and **was** (**It is I**).

**I been**   The correct way to say this is **I have been.**

**index**   The preferred plural form of this word is **indexes,** except in mathematics, where **indices** is common.

**individual**   Should not be used indiscriminately for "Person." **Person** may be applied to anyone as a general term. An individual is a particular being.

**infamous**   Pronounced **in'•fi•mus,** this word means "disgraceful, having a bad reputation." It does not mean *"unknown."*

**innovation**   Do not put *new* in front of this word: If something is innovative, it already is new.

**invaluable**   "Too valuable to be measured." Do not use when you mean **valuable.**

**invent**   "To originate something." Compare with DISCOVER.

**invite**   A verb. Do not use as a noun; that is, you receive an **invitation,** not an *invite.*

**join together**   Just say **join.** You don't need to add *together.* (The use of **join together** *is* acceptable in marriage ceremonies.)

**kind**   Say **that kind** or **those kinds.** Do not say *those kind.*

**knot** This word has several meanings, one of which is "a unit of speed." The words *an hour* should never follow it. A ship can travel at six knots or at six nautical miles per hour, but *not* at *six knots per hours.*

**kudos** Pronounced **koo'dahs** or **koo'dos.** This Greek word means "glory or fame." The final **s** is not the sign of a plural: no such thing exists as *a kudo.* **Kudos** is singular: **Kudos was due the first astronaut.**

**lay/lie** In the present tense, the verb **lay** needs an object: **Hens lay eggs. Lay the book on the table.** Lay is also the *past* tense of the verb **lie,** meaning "to assume a reclining position." **I want to lie down. Please lie down. I lay down yesterday.** (If the verb **lie** refers to the telling of a falsehood, the past tense is **lied,** as in **he lied to me.**)

**learn** Do not use *learn* when you mean **teach.** A student learns. A teacher teaches. You cannot *learn* someone how to do something, but you can teach him.

**leave** This word usually means "to depart." **Leave without me.** Do not confuse it with the word **let,** which usually means "to permit." Correct: **Let it stand the way it is. Let go of me.** But not *Leave go of me.*

**legalistic** Not interchangeable with **legal. Legalistic** implies a stricter application to the law than does **legal.**

**lend** As a verb this word is preferred over **loan.** The latter has been established as a verb in business usage; however, it is still preferable to keep the forms separate. **She asked her father for a loan, and he lent her the amount she needed.**

**less**  An adjective or an adverb meaning "not so much." **There is less milk left than I thought.** Say **fewer** when you refer to something that can be counted. See FEWER.

**liable**  Pronounced **li'•u•bl**, this word means "legally responsible, or probable (in the sense of something impending, usually dangerous or unpleasant)." **Reckless motorists are liable to suffer injuries.** Do not use as a substitute for LIKELY.

**like**  Equally, in the same manner. Use **like** before nouns or pronouns. Do not substitute *as*, which is used before a phrase or clause. See AS.

**likely**  "Probable." **The moon is likely to come out tonight.** The word has no negative connotation, as does LIABLE.

**lines of communication**  Usually preferred over *line of communication*.

**lit**  The latest dictionaries sanction this usage as a past tense form of **to light**, although **lighted** remains the more accepted form. **Lit** is all right when used as an adjective: **The candles are lit.**

**livid**  "Bluish," as a **livid** bruise.

**loan**  See LEND.

**lots of**  **Many** is preferred.

**mad**  **Mad** means "crazy or frenzied." Do not use when you mean **angry.**

**male**  Do not use as a noun. **Male** is acceptable as a noun only with reference to animals.

**maltreat, mistreat**  These two words are interchangeable.

**me**   Use it with confidence. Do not substitute *I* as the object of a verb or preposition. Say **between you and me. They came to see Bruce and me.** Do not use **me** as a subject. It is incorrect to say *Me and John are going* or *John and me are going.*

**media**   This is the plural of **medium.** Say **radio and television are popular media.** But **radio remains a popular medium.** When **medium** refers to someone with psychic abilities, the plural is **mediums.**

**mile**   It is all right to say **one mile,** but with two or more miles it is necessary to add that **s.** One may refer to a **ten-mile drive.** But do not say *I live ten mile from here.*

**most**   Do not substitute for **almost.** The misuse of *most* for **very** occurs more often in written than in spoken English, but beware of sentences like *He was most cooperative,* when "he" is not being compared with anyone.

**my**   Possessive case of the pronoun **I.** Say **This is my book.** Also say **He objected to my going.** Do not say *Do you mind me going without you?*

**myself**   You can use this word to refer *back* to yourself (**I dressed myself**) or for emphasis (**I'd rather do it myself.**) When it is incorrectly used, it hurts many ears. Wrong: *He asked Bruce and myself.* Say **He asked Bruce and me.** Wrong: *Bruce and myself are undecided.*

**never**   Means "not ever." Do not use when you mean **not.** *Who spilled the milk? I never did it!* implies that you have never in your life spilled milk.

**none**  Means "no one." Say **None of us is ready. None** is a singular subject. It demands a singular verb to match.

**nonflammable**  Since **flammable** and **inflammable** are interchangeable, use **nonflammable** to mean "will not burn."

**number**  Use **number** to refer to items that can be counted; use **amount** to refer to a general quantity. **A number of people were present. I need a large amount of sugar.** See AMOUNT.

**of**  Not a substitute for **have.** Do not say *I would of gone,* or *I wish I could of been there,* or *you shouldn't of said that.* It is **would have, could have, should have.**

**oral**  Oral means "spoken." It is not interchangeable with **verbal. Verbal** can mean "spoken" or it can refer to something that is written.

**other than**  Not *different than,* although you may say **different from.**

**out**  With **hide, win,** and **lose,** *out* is superfluous.

**over**  Instead of saying *Over forty members were there,* say **More than forty members were there.**

**over with**  Omit the *with.*

**pair, pairs**  The plural of **pair** is **pairs. I plan to take two pairs of shoes.** Never say *two pair.*

**party**  Usually refers to more than one person. Exceptions: telephone and legal usage.

**peer**  In Britain a peer is a nobleman. But in this country a peer is one who has equal standing with another. Do not use when you refer to a superior.

**people**   Preferable to *persons.*

**phase**   Means "state of transition or development." It is not to be used to mean *"aspect"* or *"topic."*

**phenomena**   This is the plural of **phenomenon**, "a visible occurrence or one that is extraordinary or marvelous." Do not use **phenomena** when speaking of only one such occurrence.

**pimento, pimiento**   Both spellings are acceptable, and both are pronounced **pi•men′•to.**

**preventative**   Preventive is preferred. Many Cincinnati doctors swear there was once a University of Cincinnati professor of preventive medicine who would flunk a student who said *preventative.*

**proved**   As the past tense of **prove**, preferred over *proven.* **It has been proved.** It is acceptable to use **proven** as an adjective: **a proven fact.**

**provided**   Preferred over *providing* when used to mean "on the condition that." **We will go provided it doesn't rain.**

**quarter of, quarter to**   When referring to time, it is correct to say **a quarter to three.** In the case of money one says **a quarter of a dollar.**

**quash**   "To put down or suppress completely." Not to be used in a milder sense. **The revolution was quashed.**

**quick**   An adjective meaning "speedy." It is not acceptable to most experts when used as an adverb. They cringe if they see or hear *Come quick.* Add the **-ly** to make it right.

**refined**   This word should not be used to describe people. Sugar is **refined.**

regard    "To consider." **Regard** also means "to hold in high esteem." It can be used to mean "reference," as in **with regard to your question.** *With regards to* is incorrect.

regards    "Greetings." This word is not considered to be interchangeable with **respect** (in the sense of **with respect to**). Nor is it interchangeable with **regard.**

relator    A **relator** narrates an account or story. Do not use when you mean **realtor,** a real estate agent affiliated with the National Association of Real Estate Boards. (Not all real estate agents are realtors.)

rob    *He robbed my pencil* is bad English. A person can be **robbed,** but his possessions are **stolen.**

run    The past tense is **ran. I ran yesterday,** not *I run yesterday.* However, it is correct to say **I have run.**

sanatarium    "A health resort." The word **sanatorium,** which used to refer to a mental institution, now can have the same meaning as **sanatarium;** however, it should be noted that there is still an aura of the old meaning hovering around **sanatorium.**

saw    One should not put **have** in front of this word. Say **I saw,** not *I have saw.* Also correct: **I have seen.** See SEEN.

scarcely    Avoid using with another negative word, as **scarcely** is already negative, and two negatives cancel each other out. Say **can scarcely,** not *can't* scarcely. Say **I can scarcely,** rather than *I can't scarcely.*

scissors    Plural in form and used with a plural verb. We usually refer to **a pair of scissors.** But **where are the scissors?**

**seen**  Avoid saying *I seen.* It is **I have seen** or **I saw.** See SAW.

**should of**  Incorrect way of saying **should have.**

**simultaneous**  Do not use to describe an action, but only to describe a thing or things. It is a simultaneous occurrence if two things happen simultaneously.

**sinus**  Something everybody has—so do not announce that you *have sinus.* You probably mean that you are having sinus inflammation or sinus discomfort.

**snuck**  No. The past tense of **sneak** is **sneaked. He sneaked around the house.**

**strata**  The plural form of **stratum.** It means "layers." You may refer to **every stratum of society,** but you would say **all strata of society.**

**suite**  Pronounced **sweet.** It means "a succession of related things: a series of connected rooms; a matched set of furniture." Please note: You may have a suit of clothes, but you own a **suite** of furniture.

**suspicion**  If you suspect something, you have a suspicion. Do not say *I suspicion.*

**swum**  The past tense of **I swim** is **I swam,** or you may say **I have swum.** You may also use **swum** when speaking of distance to be swum.

**take**  Use **take** to indicate movement away from the speaker. Example: **Take the book to him.** Compare with BRING.

**temperature**  **Tem′•pur•ah•chur.** The degree of hotness or coldness. Since everybody has one, it sounds a bit naïve to announce brightly, **I have a temperature.** If you want to tell us about it, report on whether it is above or below normal. Or simply say **I have a fever.**

**tract**    Do not say *tract* when you mean track.

**transpire**    Careful writers do not use **transpire** when they mean *happen* or *come to pass.* **Transpire** means "to be revealed, to become known," as in **We had to wait until after the war for the secret to transpire.**

**trivia**    Plural. It is wrong to say, *I don't enjoy talking about this trivia,* and *these trivia* sounds stilted. **These trivial matters** is all right. But if it's the what's-the-name-of-Buck-Rogers'-horse variety you're talking about, you're better off keeping away from all words that require a singular or plural form. No one ever says *a trivium,* either.

**try and**    Say **try to** rather than *try and;* for example, **Try to come along.** See AND.

**unawares**    The word does not have an **s.** Say **unaware.**

**undersigned**    This word seems stuffy to most people, but it is perfectly acceptable, so use it where indicated—usually only in written legal documents or other official letters or agreements.

**unique**    Means "the only one of its kind." It is incorrect to say *most unique* or *very unique.*

**up**    This is standard English, but it frequently *turns up* when not needed. Words such as **add, head, start, think,** and **wait** are stronger when you don't put **up** after them. It doesn't belong before **until** either.

**utilize**    To "utilize something" is to "find use for something already in service or to expand productivity by finding new uses." Do not substitute **utilize** for **use** if it does not have one of these meanings.

**valuable**  "Having value." Compare with INVALU-ABLE.

**via**  The meaning is usually restricted to **by way of,** rather than *by means of.*

**virus**  You can't *have a virus* the way you **have a cold.** A virus is smaller than a germ, and when you're ill with a virus attack, you may have many more than one virus.

**wait on**  Do not use when you mean **wait for.** A valet may **wait on** his master, but you do not *wait on* a friend unless you are serving him. Say **I am waiting for him.**

**way**  Take care to say **a way** when your meaning is singular: **Phyllis has a long way to go.** Add the **s** only when you refer to more than *one* way: **There are two ways to look at it.**

**went**  *Have* should never appear in front of **went. I went,** or **I have gone.**

**wore out**  It is all right to say **I wore out my shoes.** It is not acceptable to say *I'm wore out.* Say **I'm worn out,** or, better still, **I'm tired.**

**would**  Almost everyone deplored the use of *would of* for **would have,** and of *if he would have* for **if he had.**

**wrench**  "A tool." Or, if used as a verb, it means to "twist violently." It does not mean to "rinse."

**Xmas**  Although **X** represents the Greek letter **chi,** a symbol for Christ, this abbreviation is offensive to some Christians.

**yet**  Use only when it increases the clarity of a sentence; avoid the unnecessary *yet.* It is better to say **Have you washed?** than *Have you washed yet?*

**yourself**    **Yourself** is not interchangeable with **you.** It is right to say I plan to invite Gloria and you, and wrong to say *I plan to invite Gloria and yourself*. See MYSELF.

# UNMATCHED PAIRS

Many of these word couples have nothing in common but their sound, whereas some are similar in meaning but not identical. Learn to distinguish them and you will have found another way of improving your spoken English.

abjure/adjure   To **abjure** something is to "repudiate or renounce" it. **Adjure** means "command or entreat."

adverse/averse   **Adverse** means "detrimental in design or effect": **The medication caused an adverse reaction. Averse** means "strongly disinclined."

advice/advise   One offers **advice** (noun) when one **advises** (verb).

affect/effect   **Affect** means to "influence." The result is an **effect.** (By the way, there is a noun **affect** in psychology, meaning a "feeling or emotion." It is pronounced with the accent on the first syllable.)

allude/elude   **Allude** means "refer obliquely." **Elude** means to "evade."

allusion/illusion   An **allusion** is an indirect reference. Don't confuse with **illusion:** "an unreal image, a false impression." And never use **allusion** for a direct reference; just say **reference.**

alternately/   To **alternate** is to "go back and forth

**alternatively**  between two things"; thus, **alternately** means "as an occasional substitute." An **alternative** is an "option," and is the proper word to introduce a second, or even third, possibility. See ALTERNATIVE, in Usage section.

**assure/ensure**  To **assure** is "to state with confidence that something has been or will be accomplished." **Ensure** is to "make certain of something." (**Insure** is reserved for the insurance-company kind of **insure**.)

**avenge/revenge**  To **avenge** means to "exact justice." It is often confused with the word **revenge**, which means to "retaliate." If you will remember that **revenge** and **retaliate** both start with **re-**, you won't have any more trouble with these words. The corresponding nouns are **vengeance** and **revenge**.

**beside/besides**  **Beside** means "at the side of, alongside." Do not use *of* after the word **beside**. **Besides** means "in addition to, as well as."

**biannual/biennial**  The first means "twice a year" and is interchangeable with **semiannual**. The second means "every two years."

**Calvary/cavalry**  **Calvary** is the place near Jerusalem where Christ was crucified. **Cavalry** has to do with horses. I always remember the distinction between these two by associating Calvin, the Christian reformer, with the first and the word **cavalier** with the second.

**cement/concrete**  The first is dry; the second is first wet and then dry. **Concrete** is a mixture of **cement**, sand, gravel, and water.

**censor/censure**  A **censor** is "one who examines or judges." As a verb, **censor** means to "examine or assess." A **censure** is an "expression of disapproval." As a verb, it means "to express disapproval."

**childish/childlike**　**Childish** means "of, similar to, or suitable for a child." When used to describe an adult, the word often connotes foolishness. **Childlike** is a more positive word, meaning "like, or befitting, a child; innocent."

**climactic/climatic**　**Climactic** means "pertaining to a climax." **Climatic** has to do with conditions of climate.

**collaborate/ corroborate**　Remember that the word **labor** is contained in **collaborate** and you'll remember that it means "work together." To **corroborate** is to "confirm or strengthen." **He corroborated her testimony.**

**comprise/constitute**　**Comprise** means "embrace"—there's a vivid image for you. Remember it and you'll never say *the seven people that comprise the committee.* They **constitute** it. Or, **the committee comprises seven members.**

**connive/contrive**　**Connive** originally meant (and in precise usage still means) to "shut one's eyes to a crime." Possibly by confusion with **contrive,** it has come to be misused for the perpetration of the crime itself. The right word to use for a criminal act involving plotting is **conspire.**

**contemptible/ contemptuous**　**Contemptible** means "deserving of contempt"; **contemptuous** means "having contempt for."

**continual/continuous**　**Continual** means "again and again"; **continuous,** "without interruption."

**credible/credulous**　**Credible** means "believable." **Credulous** means "gullible, ready to believe." (**Cred-**

**itable** has nothing to do with believing; it means "deserving of credit or praise.")

**deprecate/depreciate**   **Deprecate** is often misused for **depreciate**. **Deprecate** means "to seek to avert by supplication," or "to disapprove." To **depreciate** is to "lower in value." The phrase *self-deprecating remarks* is best altered to **self-belittling,** or **self-disparaging, remarks.**

**distrait/distraught**   **Distrait,** pronounced dis•trā′, means "absent-minded, inattentive." **Distraught** means "distracted, harassed."

**elicit/illicit**   To **elicit** is to "draw forth, to evoke." **Illicit** is a noun meaning "illegal or unlawful."

**emigrate/immigrate**   Remember that **immigrate** and **in** both start with an **i,** and you may remember that **immigrate** means "to go in to a country"; **emigrate,** "to leave it."

**eminent/imminent**   **Eminent** means "high in station or esteem"; **imminent** means "about to happen."

**farther/further**   **Farther** refers to measurable distance. **Their house is farther away than we thought. Further,** as an adjective, describes "a continuation, usually of time or degree." **She had further news.** (As a verb it means "to advance," as in "to further a career.")

**fiscal/physical**   **Fiscal,** pronounced **fis′•kul,** means "of or pertaining to finance." **Physical, fiz′•u•kul,** means "pertaining to the body."

**flaunt/flout**   To **flaunt** is to "show off"; to **flout** to "scorn, to scoff at, to show contempt for."

**formally/formerly**   **Formally** means "in a strict or formal manner"; **formerly** means "previously."

**healthful/healthy**   **Healthful** means "health-giving"; **healthy** means "possessing health." It is therefore erroneous to speak of a *healthy walk in the mountains or glass of milk*—these things are **healthful.**

**historic/historical**   **Historic** means "important or famous in history; having influence on history." **The walk on the moon was a historic event.** In contrast, **historical** means "based on history." You may speak of a **historical novel** or a **historical fact,** but not a *historical occurrence.*

**imply/infer**   Speakers and writers **imply** something by what they say; they do not *infer.* The listeners or readers **infer** something from the remarks of the speakers or writers. Do not say *are you inferring* when you mean **are you implying.**

**impracticable/ impractical**   **Impracticable** means "not capable of being carried out; unreasonably difficult of performance." Something that is **impractical** is "not a wise thing to implement or do."

**ingenious/ingenuous**   **Ingenious,** pronounced **in•jee′•nyus,** means "resourceful, clever, inventive, adroit." The slightly rarer **ingenuous,** *in•jen′•yoo•us,* means "frank, open, honest."

**languishing/lavishing**   The first means "fading away, growing weak," as in **He was languishing in the tropical climate. Lavishing** means "laying generously upon," often used with **praise: to lavish with praise.**

**limp/limpid**   Everyone knows what **limp** means. Beware of saying **limpid** for anything but "clear": **Her eyes were limpid jewels of blue.**

| | |
|---|---|
| **loose/lose** | **Loose,** pronounced **loos,** means "not confined or restrained; free." To **lose,** pronounced **looz,** is to "mislay," or "not to win." |
| **luxuriant/luxurious** | The first means "overgrown, as a forest; full." The second, much more common, means "rich; elegant; commodious." |
| **marital/martial** | **Marital,** pronounced **mair′•i•tul,** means "pertaining to marriage." **Martial** means "of war; suitable for war; warlike," and is pronounced **mahr′•shul.** |
| **meantime/meanwhile** | Remember "meanwhile, back at the ranch," and you won't confuse these two. **Meanwhile** is an adverb, a word used to describe an action; **meantime** is a noun. Therefore, you can't say *in the meanwhile* or *meantime, back at the ranch.* |
| **moral/morale** | **Moral,** "ethical, virtuous," is pronounced **maw′•rul. Morale, maw•ral′,** means "the state of the spirits of an individual or group." |
| **nauseated/nauseous** | **Nauseated** means "feeling nausea"; **nauseous** means "causing nausea." **It was a nauseous situation.** Do not say *I feel nauseous;* rather, say **I am nauseated.** |
| **noisome/noisy** | **Noisome** means "offensive, particularly with reference to odors." Do not use it to mean "somewhat noisy." |
| **partial/partly** | **Partial** refers to preference. It is not interchangeable with **partly.** |
| **persecute/prosecute** | Both words describe negative actions by one person toward another, but **persecute** means "to oppress, annoy, molest, bother." **Prosecute** means to "sue, indict, arraign, follow, pursue." |

| | |
|---|---|
| prostate/prostrate | The first is a gland. **Prostrate** means "stretched out, prone; powerless, resigned." By the way, don't confuse **prone** ("lying face down") with **supine** ("lying face up"). |
| purposefully/ purposely | The first means "with purpose and determination"; the second, "intentionally." |
| ravage/ravish | Both have something to do with violence, but **ravage** means "destroy" and **ravish** means "rape or violate." |
| regime/regimen | **Regime** means "rule"; **regimen** means "routine." So you don't follow a *regime of diet and exercise;* it's a **regimen.** |
| regretfully/ regrettably | **Regretfully** describes the feeling of regret; **regrettably** expresses the fact that something is worthy of regret. |
| rend/render | To **rend** is to "tear." **Render** means to "give, deliver, impart; melt." |
| tortuous/torturous | **Tortuous:** "winding, twisting, circuitous," as in **It was a tortuous road. Torturous,** less frequently used, means "painful." |
| turbid/turgid | **Turbid** means "clouded; muddied." **Turgid** means "inflated, stiff." |
| venal/venial | **Venal** means "susceptible to bribery; corruptible." Do not confuse with **venial,** which, although it sometimes has to do with describing sin, means "excusable, pardonable." |

# 3 / PRONUNCIATION PITFALLS

Pronunciation is a difficult area of speech for most of us because we don't really listen to ourselves. "Proof *heed*ing" our speech is every bit as tricky as proofreading something we've written.

Participants in my Word Watchers' Clinic assure me they have mastered pitfalls in pronunciation by following the suggestions below. You can too.

*1. Use the "buddy system." Ask your spouse (who probably has your errors on tap), a fellow student, a coworker, your child, or a friend to help you spot your mistakes. Do the same for her or him if asked.*

*2. Read each pronunciation given here as though you had never seen the word before. Remember this is a special list. It consists of mispronunciations considered errors by the hundreds of contributors to this book.*

*3. If you have access to a tape recorder, by all means use it. Hear yourself as others do. Record the correct pronunciations of words that trouble you. Practice the pronunciation until you have mastered it. You can also record talk shows or educational material and play them back to make sure you have understood every word.*

*4. Check in an unabridged dictionary the pronunciation of each new word you hear.*

*5. Make flash cards of words you frequently mispronounce. Keep the cards with you until you can pronounce each word as automatically as you say "dog" and "cat."*

This chapter is a list of words that are frequently mispronounced. Learn the ones that you have trouble with—and be honest. Then make it a lifetime habit to let no word go unturned: that is, turn those dictionary pages. Learn each new word and *practice* it until you're able to use it naturally. The rewards to your self-confidence will make it worthwhile.

# Pronunciation Key

| | | | |
|---|---|---|---|
| a | as in **dad** | ō | as in **oat** |
| ā | as in **day** | oo | as in **fool** |
| ah | as in **father** | ŏŏ | as in **look** |
| ai | as in **care** | oi | as in **boy** |
| au | as in **now** | ur | as in **her** |
| aw | as in **cross** | u | as in **luck** |
| e | as in **set** | g | as in **girl** |
| ee | as in **beet** | j | as in **jam** |
| i | as in **bit** | zh | as in **vision** |
| ī | as in **bite** | | |

**absorb**   ab•**sawrb**′ is preferred over *ab•zawb*′.

**absurd**   "Contrary to common sense; ludicrous." It's pronounced ab•**surd**′, not *ab•zurd*′.

**accessory**  "Anything that contributes in a secondary way," as **accessories** to a costume. The first **c** is pronounced as a **k: ak•ses′•saw•ree.**

**across**  **ah•craws′** There is no **t** sound in this word.

**acumen**  **a•kyoo′•men.**

**adult**  Stress the second syllable, not the first: **a•dult′.**

**aged**  When you use it as an adjective, pronounce both syllables: **an ā′•jed person.** When you use it as a verb, pronounce it as one syllable: **a person who ājd rapidly.**

**à la mode**  "To the manner, to the way." Not limited to the ice cream on top of your pie. Say **ah•lah•mōd′.**

**almond**  **ah′•muhnd.**

**alumna**  Originally Latin (feminine form of **alumnus**). "A girl or woman who has attended or been graduated from a school or college." The plural form is **alumnae** (pronounced **ah•lum•nee′**).

**alumnus**  From the Latin. "A boy or man who has attended or been graduated from a school or college." **Alumni (ah•lum•nī′)** is the plural form.

**amateur**  **am′•u•tur.** Not **am′•u•chur.**

**ambassador**  **am•bas′•u•dur.** Not *am•bas′•u•dawr.*

**anti-**  As in **antibiotic** and other words, it sounds better to say **an′•tee** than **an′•tī.**

**apricot**  **ap′•ri•caht.**

**arctic**  **ahrk′•tic.** Pronounce that **c** in the middle.

**aspirin**  **as′•pur•in.** There are three syllables to the word. Avoid the *aspern* and *asprin* pronunciations.

athletics    **ath•le'•tiks.** This word has three syllables, never four.

auxiliary    Pronounce **aug•zil'•ya•ree.** Make that four syllables.

baklava    That Middle Eastern honey-and-nut pastry is **bah•klah•vah'.**

barbiturate    Sound the second **r.**

baronet    **bar'•uh•net.** A rank, in England.

basis    Means foundation. Remember that the plural form is **bases,** pronounced **bay'•seez.**

Beaujolais    Say **bō•zhō•lā'.** This is a red table wine.

berserk    **bur•surk'.** Sound both **r**'s.

bisect    **bī•sect'.**

boatswain    Pronounced **bo'•sun.** A petty officer in charge of a ship.

borrow    Rhymes with **sorrow.** Avoid the *borry* pronunciation of the word.

bouillon    **boo'•yun.** "A clear broth or soup." Note BULLION.

bovine    Make the second syllable rhyme with **wine: bo'•vīn.** It means "like a cow."

brouhaha    **broo•hah'•hah.**

bruit    "To bruit something about" is "to tell it; to let the word travel about." Pronounced **broot**—one syllable.

brut    "Dry, as champagne." Also **broot**—pronounce the **t.**

bullion    **bul'•yun.** Gold or silver uncoined or in a mass.

cabinet    **kab'•in•et.** Three syllables.

| calliope | ka•lī′•ō•pee. A musical instrument whose pipes are sounded by steam pressure, used on riverboats and in circuses. |
|---|---|
| canapé | kan′•u•pā. "An appetizer." |
| caramel | kair′•u•mel. |
| Caucasian | kaw•kā′•zhen. |
| cerebral | ser′•u•bral. |
| chafe | chāf. To make sore by rubbing. |
| chaff | chaf. The external envelopes, or husks, of grain. |
| chasm | kaz′•um. Sound that "k." A chasm is a yawning hollow, a deep gorge. |
| chassis | shas′•ee. |
| chic | sheek, not *chick* or *shick*. |
| chimney | chim′•nee. It has two syllables, not three, and an n, not an i, after the m. |
| chiropodist | ki•rah′•pe•dist. "One who treats foot ailments." Remember to pronounce the word as though it started with a k. |
| chocolate | All right to pronounce it as you did when a child—chawk′•lit. |
| coiffure | Pronounce it kwah•fyoor′. |
| colonel | kur′•nul. |
| comely | kum′•lee. "Of pleasing appearance." Does not rhyme with homely. |
| comptroller | A variant of the word controller. Used as the title for a financial officer. Pronounce it kun•tro′•lur. |
| conch | kahnk. |
| congratulate | cun•gra′•tyoo•lāt. Be sure to sound the t in the middle of the word. |

**connoisseur**  kahn•u•sur′. A competent judge of art or in matters of taste.

**consummate**  When you use the word as a verb, pronounce it kahn′•su•māt. When you use it as an adjective, meaning "extremely skilled," say kahn′•soo•mit.

**creek**  kreek. "A small stream of water, a brook." Do not confuse with crick.

**crick**  krik (rhymes with sick). "A muscle spasm."

**cuisine**  kwi•zeen′. "Style or quality of cooking."

**culinary**  kyoo′•li•nair•ee. "Of or pertaining to cooking or the kitchen."

**data, datum**  dāt′•ah; dāt′•um. Data is the plural form of datum. Although data is widely used for both, it is comforting to know the difference.

**deaf**  def. Avoid the *deef* pronunciation.

**debacle**  dā•bah′•kul.

**December**  The word is not *Dezember*. Please do not sound a z in the pronunciation.

**decrepit**  It's a t on the end, not a d.

**dentifrice**  den′•tu•fris. Do not say *den′•tur•fris*.

**despicable**  des•pik′•u•bul. Means "contemptible."

**desultory**  de′•zul•taw•ree. "Random; now and then."

**détente**  "An agreement between nations to relax or ease aggression; its purpose is to reduce tension." Pronounce it dā•tahnt′.

**detritus**  de•trī′•tus.

**diamond**  dī′•u•mund. Let's hear all three syllables.

**diaper**  dī•u•pur. It has three syllables.

**dilettante**  di•li•tahn′•tee. One who dabbles in many things but masters none.

| | |
|---|---|
| diphtheria | **dif•thir′•ee•u.** No *dip* sound in this word. |
| dirigible | **dur′•u•ju•bl.** |
| draught | Chiefly British. Pronunciation and meaning interchangeable with **draft.** |
| dreamed, dreamt | **dreemd; dremt.** Either of these words is correct. |
| ecstasy | **ek′•stah•see.** |
| ecumenism | **ek′•yoo•mu•nizm.** |
| elm | This word has one syllable; do not make it *el′•lum.* |
| ennui | **ahn•wee′.** Means "boredom, listlessness." |
| en route | **ahn•root′.** "On or along the way." |
| entree | **ahn′•trā′.** "The right to enter," or "the main course of a meal." |
| envelope | **en′•vah•lōp** if a noun; **en•vel′•up** if a verb. |
| environment | **en•vī•run•ment.** Let's hear that **n** in the middle. |
| epicurean | **ep•u•kyoor•ee′•an.** |
| err | **ur.** |
| escape | **es•cāp′.** There is no **x** in this word. |
| espresso | **es•pres′•sō.** Not *ex•pres′•sō.* |
| et cetera | **et•set′•ur•u.** Never say *ek•set′•ur•u.* |
| experiment | **ek•spair′•u•ment.** There is no *spear* in this word. |
| faux pas | "A blunder." Say **fō•pah′,** or else you will demonstrate what it is. |
| February | **Feb′•roo•a•ree.** Please pronounce both **r**'s. |
| fiancé | **fee•ahn′•sā.** Pronounce this as you would the feminine word **fiancée.** |
| field | Be sure to sound the **d** at the end of the word. |

| | |
|---|---|
| **fifth** | There is an **f** in the middle. |
| **film** | The word has one syllable; do not say *fil'•um*. Or *flim*. |
| **fiscal** | **fis'•kul.** "Of or pertaining to finance." Do not confuse with physical. |
| **fission** | **fizh'•un.** Not **fish'•in.** |
| **flaccid** | **flak'•sid.** "Flabby." |
| **flautist, flutist** | **flau'•tist** is preferred. The first syllable rhymes with **now.** |
| **forbade** | The past tense of **forbid** is pronounced **for•bad'.** |
| **forte** | "That which one does most easily." It has one syllable (say **fawrt**); unless, of course, you're using the musical **forte** (meaning "loud"), and then you say **fawr'tā.** |
| **foyer** | **fwah•yā** was the original pronunciation, although most dictionaries accept **foy'•ur.** |
| **fracas** | **fra•kus.** "A noisy quarrel." |
| **gauche** | **gōsh.** "Clumsy, tactless." |
| **genealogy** | **jee•nee•ahl'•u•jee.** Please note the **a** in the middle of the word. |
| **genuine** | **jen'•yoo•in.** Avoid making the last syllable rhyme with **vine.** |
| **giant** | Pronounced **jī'•ant,** not *jīnt.* |
| **giblet** | **jib•lut.** |
| **government** | **gu'•vurn•ment.** Be sure to sound the **n** in the middle. |
| **granted** | **gran•ted.** One should be able to take for granted that this word will not be confused with **granite.** |
| **grievous** | **gree'•vus.** |
| **grocery** | **grō'•sir•ee.** Make it three syllables. |

| | |
|---|---|
| guarantee | gair•un•tee′. The first syllable rhymes with **air.** |
| gynecology | You pronounce the **g** as you do in **girl.** It is **gī•nu•kahl′•u•jee.** |
| hallucinogen | ha•loo′•sin•u•jen. Confusing, because in **carcinogen** the accent is on the **sin.** |
| harass | har′•us. "To disturb or irritate." The accent is preferred on the first syllable. |
| harbinger | hahr′•bin•jur. Something that is a sign of what is to come. |
| height | hīte. Rhymes with **kite.** |
| help | Let's hear that **l.** The word is **help,** not *hep.* |
| herb | The preferred pronunciation is **urb.** Note that you do sound the **h** in **herbaceous** and **herbivore.** |
| homage | Let's hear the **h**: hahm′•ij. |
| hors d'oeuvre | awr′•durv′. Please note that you do not pronounce the **s.** The French do not pronounce the final **s** when they use the plural form. "An appetizer." |
| hosiery | hō′•zher•ee. |
| hospitable | The accent is on the first syllable. |
| huge | hyooj. Let's hear the **h** at the beginning of the word. |
| human | hyoo′•mun. Always pronounce the **h.** Do not say *yoo•*mun. |
| humble | hum′•bul. That **h** is sounded. |
| humor | Sound the **h**: hyoo•mur. |
| hundred | hun′•dred. The last syllable rhymes with **Fred.** Neither *hunnert* or *hunderd* is correct. |
| hypnotize | This word has many mispronunciations. It |

is not *hit'•nu•tīze* or *hip'•mu•tīze.* Say **hip'•nu•tīz.**

**idea**    Say this aloud. Did you add an **r** to the word? It is not *idear.*

**Illinois**    **Il•u•noi'.** "Noise" in this word bothers many people.

**indict**    **in•dīt'.** Rhymes with **light.** It means "to charge (usually with a crime)."

**integral**    **in'•te•grul.** It means "essential to completeness." Make sure that the **r** is in the right place: don't say *intregal.* It is not *in•teg'•ral,* either.

**intermezzo**    **in•tur•met'•sō.**

**internecine**    **in•tur•nee'•seen.** Means "relating to a struggle within a group."

**intravenous**    **in•truh•vee'•nus.** Note that the word is not *in•ter'•venous.*

**irrevocable**    **i•rev'•u•ku•bl.** "Irreversible."

**Italian**    **I•tal'•yun.** Do not say *Eye•tal'•yun.*

**italics**    **ī•tal'•iks,** not *ī•tal'•iks.* It means "cursive print," such as the type used to designate incorrect pronunciations in this section.

**jabot**    **zhah•bō'.** A cascade of frills down the front of a shirt.

**jamb**    **jam.** Do not sound the **b.** Posts or pieces of a door or window frame.

**jewelry**    **joo'•el•ree.** It has three syllables.

**jocose**    **jō•kōs'.** "Joking."

**jocund**    **jawk'•und.** "Merry," "of cheerful disposition."

**jodhpurs**    **jod'•purz,** not *jod'•furs.* The name derives from Jodhpur, a state of India.

junta    **hoon′•tah.** Give the **j** an **h** sound. It means "a group of military officers holding state power in a country after a *coup d'état.*"

just    Rhymes with **must.** Avoid the *jest* pronunciation.

juvenile    **joo′•vu•nul.** The last syllables does not rhyme with **mile.** It means "not yet adult."

karate    **ku•rah′•tee.** "A Japanese system of unarmed self-defense." The word literally means "empty-handed."

kibbutz    **ki•bo͞ots′.** The plural form is kibbutzim: **ki•bo͞ot•seem′.** A kibbutz is a "collective farm or settlement, usually in Israel."

kiln    **Kil** is still the preferred pronunciation.

kindergarten    **kin′•dur•gahr•tn.** It is not *kindergarden* or *kinny garden.*

kirsch    **kirsh.** Originally, "a colorless brandy made from the fermented juice of cherries."

knew    Pronounce **nyoo.**

knish    Dough filled with meat or potato. Pronounce the **k.**

known    One syllable please: **nōn.**

lackadaisical    My favorite baseball manager is one of the many people who mispronounce this word. Pronounce it **lak•a•dā•zi•kul,** with no **s** in the second syllable.

lambaste    **lam•bāst′.** Slang. To beat soundly, to scold severely.

larynx    **lar′•ingks.** It is not *lahr′•nicks.*

least    Pronounce the **t.**

length    **lengkth.** Avoid the *lenth* pronunciation.

liable    **lī′•u•bl.** Three syllables, in order not to confuse it with libel.

liaison "A connecting link." It's pronounced **lee•ā'•zahn**, not *lee•u•zahn*.

library **lī'•brair•ee.** Please pronounce the **r** in the middle.

long-lived **lawng•līvd'**, not *lawng•līvd'*.

machinate **mak'•i•nāt.** "To plot or to devise a plot."

maniacal "Insane." Pronounce it **me•nī'•u•kul.**

manufacture **man•yoo•fak'•chur.** Be sure to sound the **u** in the middle of this word.

marinade **mar•u•nād'.**

marshmallow The chances are good that if you spell it correctly, you will also say it correctly. It is **marsh'•mal•lō.**

mêlée **mā'•lā.** "A confusing fracas."

menstruate The word has three syllables: not *men'•strāte.*

mezzanine **mez'•u•neen.**

milieu **meel•yu'.** "Surroundings, environment."

miniature **min'•ee•u•choor.** Please pronounce all four syllables. I still prefer the **t** sound for the last syllable, but most modern dictionaries give it the **ch** sound.

minutia **mi•noo'•shee•u.** A small or relatively unimportant detail. The plural of this word is **minutiae** and you pronounce it **mi•noo'•shee•ee.**

mischievous **mis'•chi•vus.** Three syllables only.

mnemonics **ni•mahn'•iks.** This is a plural noun, but it is used with a singular verb. It means a system to improve or develop the memory.

modern **mahd'•urn.** Please do not say *modren.*

| | |
|---|---|
| motor | mō•tur. That is a **t** in the middle. |
| mousse | moos. "A light dessert." |
| muenster | mŏŏn'•stur. |
| notary public | Not *notory republic.* |
| nuclear | noo'•klee•ur. The late President Eisenhower said *noo'•kyu•lur,* but of course no one outranked him, so his pronunciation went uncorrected. |
| offertory | The word has four syllables. Please note: There is no **a** in the middle of the word. |
| often | off'•n. The **t** is silent. |
| once | wuhns. This is a one syllable word, without a **t.** |
| only | ōn'•lee. Do not say *olny.* |
| ophthalmologist | It means "eye doctor." It's **ahf•thal•mahl'•u•gist.** |
| orgy | or'•jee. It means "unrestrained indulgence." |
| particular | pahr•tik'•yoo•lur. Be sure to sound all four syllables. |
| patina | pat'•u•nu. "A shine or luster, or a coat of oxidation, as on brass or copper." |
| perfume | pur'•fyoom is preferred. |
| permanent | pur'•mu•nent. Do not reverse the **m** and the **n.** |
| persevere | Don't add an extra **r** before the **v.** |
| perspiration | pur•spur•ā'•shun. The first syllable is **per,** not *pre.* A recent commercial presented a fashion designer who mispronounced this word. |
| petit | pet'•ee. Used in law. It means "minor" or "petty." |

petite      pu•teet'. "Small, trim."

piano       pee•an'•ō. Avoid the pī•a•no pronuncia-
            tion. Also avoid changing the final o to an
            a.

picture     pik'•chur. Be sure to sound the k sound.
            *Pitch'•ur* is an unacceptable pronunciation
            for this word.

piquant     pee'•kunt. "Having an agreeably pungent
            or tart taste; provocative."

piquante    pee•kahnt'. Same meaning as above.

plagiarize  plā'•ju•rīze. Use a j in the middle, not a g
            as in **girl**.

poem        po'•em. Make that two syllables. No
            *pomes*, please.

poetry      po'•e•tree. Sound all three syllables.

poignant    poin'•yent. "Distressing."

poinsettia  poin•set'•ee•u.

porcine     pawr'•sīn. "Like a pig."

posthumous  pahs'•choo•mus. "Occurring or continuing
            after death."

précis      prā•see'. "A summary." Don't be confused
            by the accent.

prelude     The preferred pronunciation is **prel'•yood**.

pretzel     prets'•l. Be sure to begin with a p.

proboscis   prōbahs'•is. A long snout, like an anteat-
            er's. Don't pronounce the c.

prohibition prō•i•bi'•shun. The h is silent.

protein     You may say **pro'•teen** or **pro'•tee•in**.

proviso     prō•vī'•sō. "A limiting clause in a
            contract."

pumpkin     pump'•kin.

| | |
|---|---|
| quasi | kwa'•zi. "To some degree, almost, somewhat." |
| quay | kee. A wharf. |
| quiche | keesh. "A custard, often with bacon and cheese, baked in an unsweetened pastry crust." |
| quiescent | kwē•es'•unt. "Still; silent." |
| quiet | kwī'•it. This word has two syllables. |
| radiator | rā'•dee•ā•tur. |
| rapport | ra•por'. The t on the end of the word is silent. |
| ration | You may say rash'•un or rā'•shun. |
| recognize | The word is rek'•ug•nīz. Be sure the g in the middle is heard. |
| relapse | Most people use ree•laps' for the verb and ree'•laps for the noun, but ree•laps' is correct for both. |
| relator | The word you want is realtor. Pronounce it ree'•ul•tr and not ree•lā•tr. Note that the a comes before the l. Refers to a real-estate agent affiliated with the National Association of Real Estate Boards. |
| relevant | rel'•u•vent. The l comes before the v. |
| remembrance | ree•mem'•bruns. Three syllables. Please do not say ree•mem'•ber•ans. |
| reservoir | re'•zur•vwah. |
| restaurant | res'•tawr•ahnt. The word has three syllables, not two. |
| résumé | "A summing up." Pronounce it re'•zoo•mā or rā'•zoo•mā. |
| Revelation | The last book in the New Testament is Revelation (without an s). |
| revenue | re'•ven•yoo, not re'•ven•oo. |

rinse     **rins.** Do not say *wrench* for **rinse.**

robust    It means "strong, healthy," and it's pronounced **ro•bust′.**

roof      Pronounce it **roof,** not *ruf.*

root beer The **root** rhymes with **boot,** not *book.*

rosé      **rō•zā′.** "A wine that is suitable for either white or dark meat; it is pink in color."

route     Pronounce either **root** or **rowt.** The pronunciation **root** is given first in most dictionaries.

saboteur  **sab•u•ter′.**

sacrilegious **sak•ru•lee′•jus.** "Irreverent."

sadism    **sad′•izm.**

sauterne  **sō•tairn′.** "A white table wine."

schism    **siz′•em.** "A separation."

scion     **si′•en.** "A descendant or heir."

sexual    **sek′•shoo•ul.** Not **seks′•yoo ul.**

sherbet   **sher′•bit.** Note that it is not *sherbert.*

shown     **shōn.** One syllable.

similar   **sim′•i•ler.** "Resembling." Do not pronounce it **sim′•yoo•ler.**

sink      As it's spelled—not *zink.*

soiree    **swah•rā′.** "A party."

solder    **sahd′•r.** The l is silent.

soprano   Be sure to sound an **o** at the end of the word (it does not end with **a**).

sotto voce **sawt′•ō•vō•chee.** "Very softly; in an undertone."

species   **spee′•sheez.**

strength  **strengkth.** Do not say *strenth.*

suite      Pronounce it **sweet**. It means "a succession of related things; a series of connected rooms; a matched set of furniture." (Please note: you may have a suit (**soot**) of clothes, but you do not have a suit of furniture.)

surprise      **sur•prīz'**. Note that the pronunciation is not *suh'•prīz*.

table d'hôte      **taw'•blu•dōt** (literally, "table of the host"). "Meal of the house served at a fixed price."

tarot      **ta•rō'**.

temperamental      This word has five syllables. Be sure to sound both the **er** and the **a** syllables in the middle of the word.

temperature      **tem'•pur•u•chur**. Pronounce all four syllables.

theater      **thee'•u•tur**. Do not say *thee•ā'•tur*.

thorough      **thur'•ō**. Never put an **l** in this word (making it *thorul*).

tired      **tīrd**.

toward      **Tawrd** is the preferred pronunciation in the United States.

tract      Do not say **tract** when you mean **track**.

Tuesday      It is **tyooz'•dā**, say the purists; **tooz'•dā** now appears in many dictionaries.

umbrella      **um•brel'•u**.

unaware      Make sure that you do not add an **s** to the end of this word.

undoubtedly      **un•dau'•ted•lee**. Do not pronounce the **b** in **doubt**.

valet      **val'•et**.

vapid      **vap'•id**. "Tasteless, dull."

| | |
|---|---|
| vaudeville | vōd′•vil. |
| vehement | vee′•u•ment. The h remains silent. |
| veterinarian | vet•ur•u•nar′•ee•un. There are six syllables. The word *vet* is not pleasing to most veterinarians. |
| via | Either vī′•u or vee′•u is correct. (The meaning is usually restricted to "by way of"; "by means of" is not an accepted meaning.) |
| viaduct | vī′•u•dukt. Note that it is not *vī′•u•dahk*. |
| vice versa | You may say vī′•see•vur′•su OR vīs′•vur′•su. I no longer laugh inwardly when I hear that first pronunciation. That's the way many experts say it. |
| vichyssoise | vee′•shee•swahz. Pronounce the final s as a z. |
| victuals | vit′•ls. "Food." |
| vignette | vin•yet′. "Ornamental design; a picture; a short literary composition." |
| virago | vi•rā′•gō. "A bad-tempered woman." |
| voyeur | vwah•yur′. |
| wash | Please do not say *wawrsh*. There is no r in the word. |
| Washington | The first syllable does not have an r in it. |
| Westminster | No *minister* here, please. |
| whale | There is an h in the word. It is pronounced |

hwāl, or rhyme with **mail**.

| | |
|---|---|
| **what** | **hwaht**. Sound the **h**. |
| **when** | **hwen**. Sound the **h**. |
| **where** | **hwair**. Sound the **h**. And the word rhymes with **care**, not *car*. |
| **which** | **hwich**. Sound the **h**. |
| **while** | **hwīl**. Sound the **h**. |
| **white** | **hwīt**. Sound the **h**. |
| **with** | Pronounce the **th** as you do in father. |
| **wrestle** | Not *ras'•sel*. |
| **Xavier** | **Zā'•vee•ur**. |
| **yellow** | Avoid the *yella* pronunciation. |
| **zoology** | **zō•ahl'•u•jee**. The first syllable rhymes with **go** rather than with *to*. |

# Now a Word from You, Please

If I have failed to include your pet phobia, please let me know. Copy the form on page 81 onto a postcard and mail it to me,

*Mrs. Phyllis Martin*
*c/o David McKay Company*
*750 Third Avenue*
*New York, N.Y. 10017*

Mrs. Martin:

You failed to include my pet phobia.

How about _____?          And shouldn't _____

be _____?

Suggestion for your next edition: _____

_____

Signed: (if you wish) _____

Student_____ Education_____     Age: under 21_____

Occupation_____ Sex_____          over 21_____